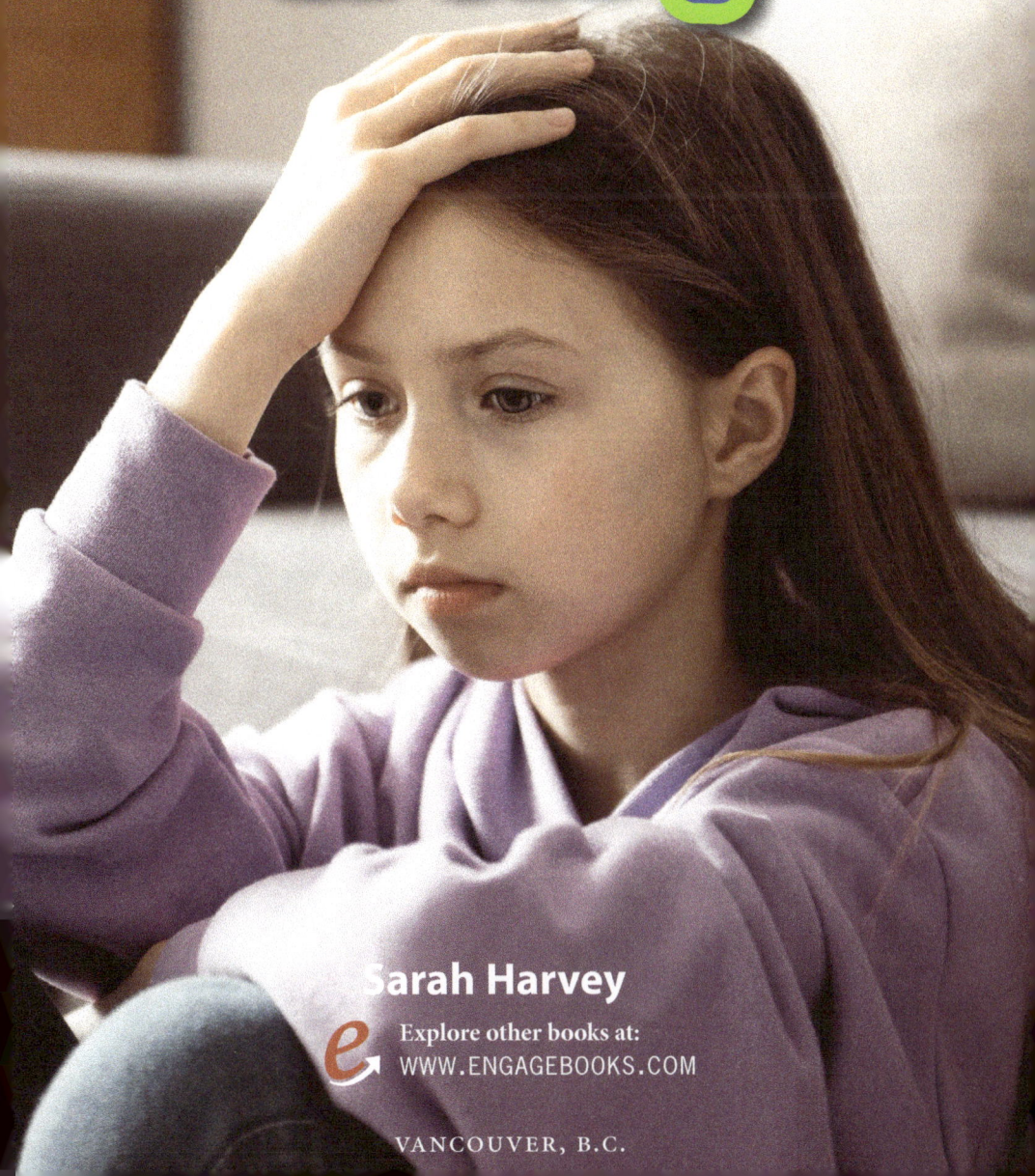

EMOTIONS and FEELINGS

Worry

Sarah Harvey

Explore other books at:
WWW.ENGAGEBOOKS.COM

VANCOUVER, B.C.

e WWW.ENGAGEBOOKS.COM

Worry: Level 2
Emotions and Feelings
Harvey, Sarah N. 1950 –
Text © 2023 Engage Books
Design © 2023 Engage Books

Edited by: A.R. Roumanis, Ashley Lee, Melody Sun,
and Sarah Harvey
Design by: Mandy Christiansen

Text set in Arial Regular.
Chapter headings set in Arial Black.

FIRST EDITION / FIRST PRINTING

LIBRARY AND ARCHIVES CANADA CATALOGUING IN PUBLICATION

Title: Worry / Sarah Harvey.
Names: Harvey, Sarah N., 1950- author.
Description: Series statement: Emotions and feelings

Identifiers: Canadiana (print) 2023044735x | Canadiana (ebook) 20230447368
ISBN 978-1-77878-150-6 (hardcover)
ISBN 978-1-77878-151-3 (softcover)
ISBN 978-1-77878-152-0 (epub)
ISBN 978-1-77878-153-7 (pdf)
ISBN 978-1-77878-154-4 (audio)

Subjects:
LCSH: Worry—Juvenile literature.
LCSH: Worry in children—Juvenile literature.

Classification: LCC BF723.W67 H37 2023 | DDC J155.4/1246—DC23

This project has been made possible in part
by the Government of Canada.

Canada

Contents

4   What Is Worry?

6   Why Do People Worry?

8   Are There Different Kinds of Worry?

10   How Does Worry Affect the Way You Think?

12   How Does Worry Affect the Way You Act?

14   Can Worry Be a Good Thing?

16   Does Everyone Worry?

18   What Does Worry Feel Like?

20   Can You Stop Feeling Worried?

22   Does Worry Ever Go Away?

24   Does Worry Change as You Grow Older?

26   What Can You Do if You Feel Worried?

28   What Can You Do if Other People Feel Worried?

30   Quiz

What Is Worry?

Worry is an emotion that makes you feel uneasy or fearful about events in your life. Worry is a normal and healthy emotion.

COVID-19 caused the whole world to worry. It made people be very careful.

4

Being worried about a lot of things at the same time is called **anxiety**. Not all worry leads to anxiety.

5

Why Do People Worry?

Worrying is the mind's way of trying to deal with danger. The danger may be real or it may not.

Some people think worrying can stop bad things from happening. Worrying cannot change the future. Only action can.

A monster in the closet is not real, but it may feel very real to a toddler.

Are There Different Kinds of Worry?

Practical worries are things people can act on. You might be worried about a math test. If you study hard, you will not be so worried. And you might get a really good mark.

People often worry about things they cannot control. There is nothing you can do about the weather on your vacation. Worrying about it will not help.

How Does Worry Affect the Way You Think?

Worried people think about all the ways things can go wrong. It is very hard to stop thinking this way. Too much worry can lead to **depression**.

KEY WORD

Depression: strong feelings of sadness and lack of hope.

Worrying makes small things seem bigger than they are. If you get sick, you might worry that you are missing too much school. Then you might worry about falling behind.

How Does Worry Affect the Way You Act?

Worry can make people too afraid to act. You may believe you cannot make things better. This can make you not want to try.

Worry can stop you from making decisions. You may worry you will make the wrong one. No one makes the right decision every time.

Making the wrong decision can teach you how to make better decisions in the future.

Can Worry Be a Good Thing?

Worry can help us take action to solve our problems. Many people are worried about **endangered** animals. Their worry can lead them to take action to help protect these animals.

KEY WORD

Endangered: an animal population that is at risk of dying off.

14

Being worried you cannot swim can help you decide to take swimming lessons. Being worried about a friend can make you check in on them.

Does Everyone Worry?

Everyone worries sometimes. This is normal. **Sensitive** people worry more.

Some people do not worry much. They focus on the present, not the future. They may have just been born that way.

Asking "what if" questions can be a sign you are worrying about the future.

What Does Worry Feel Like?

Worrying can cause you to feel **stress**. You might feel afraid or confused. Some people have a hard time sitting still when they worry.

KEY WORD

Stress: when people feel uncomfortable about something that is happening.

An adult can help you deal with your stress.

Worrying can make your stomach feel upset. You might get a headache or feel very tired. You might find it difficult to move your body.

Can You Stop Feeling Worried?

It can be hard to stop worrying. Your thoughts can go around and around in a loop. Thinking about something happy or hopeful can help you get out of the loop.

Think about your helmet protecting you if you are worried about falling off your bike.

If you find you cannot stop worrying, talk to an adult. They may be able to help you or take you to a doctor.

Does Worry Ever Go Away?

There will always be things in life that worry you. Worry comes and goes for most people. Worrying from time to time is normal.

Extreme anxiety often does not go away. Getting help from a doctor or **therapist** can help make anxiety less scary. People may need to take medicine to help them feel better.

Does Worry Change as You Grow Older?

What people worry about changes as they grow older. Young children may worry about being away from their family. They may worry about being left out by their friends.

Older children might worry about not doing well at school. Some adults learn how to deal with worry in a healthy way. They can help their children do the same.

If your family worries a lot, you may find it hard not to worry.

What Can You Do if You Are Worried?

Try to breathe slowly. Focus on what is real, not on what might happen. Talk to a trusted adult about what is worrying you.

Avoiding your worries can make them worse.

Think about what you can and cannot control. You cannot control whether the kids at your new school will like you or not. But you can control how nice you are to them.

What Can You Do if Other People Are Worried?

Do something to **distract** a friend if they are worried about something they cannot control. Play a game together or watch a movie.

KEY WORD

Distract: draw attention away from something.

Help them focus on the present. Remind them that worrying is normal. You may not be able to stop a friend from worrying, but you can still be there for them.

Quiz

Test your knowledge of worry by answering the following questions. The questions are based on what you have read in this book. The answers are listed on the bottom of the next page.

1 What is anxiety?

2 What are practical worries?

3 Does everyone worry?

4 What can too much worrying lead to?

5 Is it easy to stop worrying?

6 Can avoiding your worries make them worse?

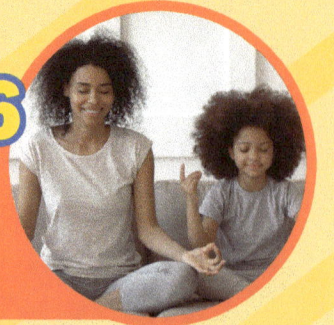

Explore other books in the Emotions and Feelings series.

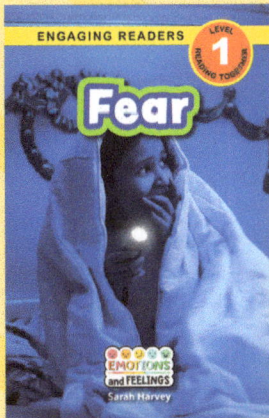

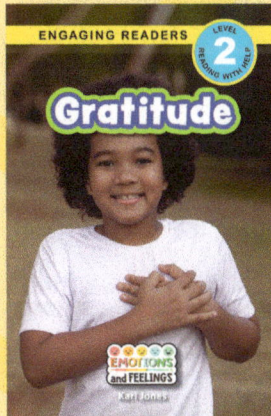

ENGAGING READERS — LEVEL 1 — READING TOGETHER
Fear
EMOTIONS and FEELINGS
Sarah Harvey

ENGAGING READERS — LEVEL 1 — READING TOGETHER
Happiness
EMOTIONS and FEELINGS
Kari Jones

ENGAGING READERS — LEVEL 1 — READING TOGETHER
Sadness
EMOTIONS and FEELINGS
Sarah Harvey

ENGAGING READERS — LEVEL 1 — READING TOGETHER
Surprise
EMOTIONS and FEELINGS
Kari Jones

ENGAGING READERS — LEVEL 2 — READING WITH HELP
Gratitude
EMOTIONS and FEELINGS
Kari Jones

ENGAGING READERS — LEVEL 2 — READING WITH HELP
Grief
EMOTIONS and FEELINGS
Sarah Harvey

ENGAGING READERS — LEVEL 2 — READING WITH HELP
Guilt
EMOTIONS and FEELINGS
Sarah Harvey

ENGAGING READERS — LEVEL 2 — READING WITH HELP
Love
EMOTIONS and FEELINGS
Sarah Harvey

ENGAGING READERS — LEVEL 2 — READING WITH HELP
Worry
EMOTIONS and FEELINGS
Sarah Harvey

Visit www.engagebooks.com/readers

www.ingramcontent.com/pod-product-compliance
Lightning Source LLC
Chambersburg PA
CBHW051241020426

42331CB00016B/3480